WISDOM FROM SPIRIT GUIDES

HEALING THE HUMAN EGO

by
Lynn A. Walker

The Light of Our Being
Minneapolis, MN
www.thelightofourbeing.org

WISDOM FROM
SPIRIT GUIDES

HEALING THE HUMAN EGO

By Lynn A. Walker

All rights reserved.

COPYRIGHT © 2015 Rev. Lynn A. Walker

Cover Designer: Dreamz
Layout Designer: Carla Green, Studio C Graphics
Editors: Karen Goodman and Carol McDonald

No part of this book may be reproduced in any form or by any electronic or mechanical means including information storage and retrieval systems, without permission in writing from the author. The only exception is by a reviewer, who may quote short excerpts in a review or brief quotations in articles.

First Printing: 2015

ISBN Hard Cover:	978-0-9909017-3-0
ISBN Paperback:	978-0-9909017-0-9
ISBN eBook:	978-0-9909017-1-6
ISBN Audiobook:	978-0-9909017-2-3

The Light of Our Being Publishing
PO Box 26394
Minneapolis, MN 55426

About the Author

Rev. Lynn A. Walker
Founder & President
The Light of Our Being
Visit www.thelightofourbeing.org

THIS BOOK SERIES IS ABOUT YOU AND ME as spiritual beings. It's about us as a global nation. It's about wisdom from Spirit Guides that make us open our minds, change our perspectives and move us to heal ourselves so that we can heal others.

I've communicated with my Spirit Guides since childhood. I can hear them, sense them, and see them. I never questioned their existence and because I'm open, I've experienced different phenomena. That makes me 'strange' in the eyes of some that are amused, and 'crazy' according to the opinions of those threatened. Those that also communicate with their guides know what I mean. Spirit Guides tell it like it is without ego manipulations. I always value their input especially when they give me insight into our evolvement.

When I was young, I thought everyone could at least hear their Guides until my mother told me to stop telling things that I heard. I realized when I got older that she was trying to protect me, but I'm glad I didn't listen to her – at least for any significant length of time.

They say psychic powers skip a generation. My mother admitted that her mother 'knew' things before they would happen. All people have communicated with their Spirit Guides – without exception. Most do not realize when they have.

Since my early teens I studied many metaphysical topics including astrology, the Natural Laws, vibrational energy, spiritual anatomy, and channeling under various teachers living and in the spirit world. A Reiki Master since 1988, I also hold a bachelor's degree in chemistry and an MBA.

Ordained in 2003 after seven years of study and an additional 10 years of personal growth, I started The Light of Our Being to answer my calling to help others on the path. I realize my books and classes aren't for everyone but regardless, these works now need to be made public. The era of withholding spiritual knowledge is over.

When I began to realize that science is currently verifying ancient metaphysical teachings, my goal has been to bring the two together as I teach so that people can understand their reality and harness their own true potential.

When I'm not teaching, counseling, or guest lecturing, you'll find me reading or pursuing short and long distance adventures mentally and physically.

Visit www.thelightofourbeing.org to see the upcoming seminar schedule on various topics and online resources for personal growth.

You can email me your thoughts or experiences with this book at my personal email address lynn@lynnwalker.org .

Dedication

This book is a compilation of channeled classes dealing with the state of the human ego through channels Rev. Lynn A. Walker (the author) and Rev. Roseann M. Wagers (teacher and advisor).

My eternal, heartfelt gratitude goes to my Spirit Guides for their dedicated help, limitless patience, and perseverance with me in this incarnation. (Believe me, they haven't had an easy job!) My never ending appreciation and love goes to Cornelius, Phoebe, Martin, Catherine, He Nu, Leonard and Albert Michaelson, White Hawk, White Moon, Mikael, Carmen, Rose, Iris, Omar, Wagner, Carolyn, Marilyn, teachers, wise women, and friends that have been so kind and supportive.

Rev. Roseann M. Wagers
1943 – 2014
Great Incarnation!
RIP

Gregory S. Grigsby
1947 – 2015
One That Inspired Many
RIP

Contents

About the Author iii

Dedication v

Contents. vii

Foreword ix

Introduction 1

The Predator. 5

Ways of the Predator 11

Humbling the Predator 21

The Table of Emotional Understanding 27

The Balanced Ego 37

Exercise 1: Working With Your Emotions. 39

Exercise 2: What Do You Think of Yourself? 43

Foreword

I PREVIOUSLY WROTE A PAMPHLET about a similar topic but was told by Spirit that it was a prelude to a much larger theme that they referred to as 'the human ego from a spiritual perspective'.

The greater part of the contents of this first book of the series came to me the morning of September 4, 2014 at 1:32 am when my Spirit Guides awakened me. They were ready to work, so I got out of bed. From past experiences (yes plural) I knew better than to argue no matter how tired I was. The book was done in time for me to shower and go to work that same morning. And, I didn't feel tired all day.

My Spirit Guides had a lot to say concerning the egos of humans that morning. This book details their perspective. They often referred to the personality/ego as "the Predator" in class discussions. The personality is a vehicle for the ego. According to them, the personality/ego is represented as the devil in the Bible. It is what keeps us separate from our oneness with our Higher Self that is God. I'm not a psychologist but I gained more insight from them about the human psyche over the years than I ever read in any psychology book.

Over the years, the numerous Spirit Guides that instructed the classes were very patient with us. We were chided when we did things we knew we shouldn't. (After all, they were training future teachers.) We were also pushed to explore levels of consciousness beyond our perceived limitations, or what they called our "ring-past-not." They empowered us through teaching the Universal Natural Laws (*Kybalion* by the Three Initiates) in a very practical and relatable sense using our own experiences.

We are living in times of great fear and unrest. It is my hope that this book will empower you as you walk your path. The first step towards enlightenment is dealing with the Predator – your personality/ego.

Introduction

I REALLY DIDN'T UNDERSTAND what an ego was. In college, I took a psychology course and became aware that there are many interpretations of the ego, but it didn't sink into my brain. During my ministerial training classes in my late twenties, I was confronted by my ego, my own Predator as Spirit called it.

In short, life underneath the mask of the business person/chemist was daunting. The facade looked wonderful but I was having relationship issues, family issues, and strained friendships. Years prior, I was raped two months after arriving on my college campus at age 17, had a dysfunctional childhood, a violently abusive father (with undiagnosed psychological issues), a mother that feared her husband, and the list goes on. I was always angry and trusted no one but myself, my Spirit Guides, and the mother of my best friend. My Guides and my friend's mother were my 'relief valves'. I don't know where I'd be without them. I repressed my emotions to protect myself. However, the emotions started to surface when I moved halfway across the country to live on my own.

Through years of sometimes painful self-awareness sessions during my ministerial training and some years after, I finally got an astonishing look at my own ego. It took a while to peel back the protective layers that covered it, but with the help of my personal Spirit Guides I was able to stay in a connected meditative state and watch my personality/ego at work.

The best way I can describe this is that I was consciously in my higher mind objectively observing myself. I've had out-of-body experiences, but this wasn't it. It was similar. This made me realize how much I identified my personality/ego as being "me." I know now that it isn't. My personality/ego is simply "clothing" that I'm wearing in this incarnation called "Lynn." However, it was a surprise to me at the time that my personality "Lynn" is not my spiritual identification. It was the first time I became conscious of the illusion.

> ..but my Spirit Guides say it's the journey that's important, not the destination.

During that entire period, I observed myself from a lofty birds-eye-view over several weeks. I observed my personality/ego (my Predator) looking for validation in various ways. It is my Predator that needed this outer world, the earth plane illusion, to prove its worth and to justify its existence. It is the Predator that needed to justify "Lynn" and my Predator was running on empty.

In retrospect, that experience was a real awakening for me. Being consciously aware of my Predator alleviated the stress that I placed on others and myself, and quieted my inner critic. I'm calmer, more patient, and more focused than I used to be and much more at peace with just being. And, to my surprise, inner happiness followed a feeling of connectedness to my Higher Self. Yes, I still have frustrations and setbacks, but they are now in perspective and I choose from my higher mind how to respond and how to transmute the situation. I'm not the type that puts on rose colored glasses and thinks everything is flowery and wonderful. Iris (Spirit Guide) always told us that avoidance is not spiritual. I have karma to work on while I'm on this earth plane as do you or you wouldn't be here. Your Spirit Guides will help you through the karma but they cannot eliminate it for you. It is yours to transmute. It's best to have a sober outlook in this illusion or you can easily get lost.

I'm not going to say it was or has continued to be an easy journey for me or that absolute bliss is at hand or instantaneous. Only my Higher Self knows of my progress and my evolution - as does yours. I learned early not to judge someone's level of consciousness by appearances because appearances can be deceiving and often are. Taming your Predator takes work, and while the journey may be easy for some, it hasn't been for me. It seems I'm taking the long road to self-awareness, but my Spirit Guides say it's the journey that's important, not the destination. That's easy for them to say. According to them, the more that I experience and transmute, the more I will be able to show others on the path. That's true for all of us. They said that I have all the time in the universe. That statement puzzled me at first until I realized time is an earth plane illusion. All paths lead to God – The All. And The All can change anything instantaneously.

> Sometimes being honest with yourself is the most difficult part.

The result of this conscious journey is freeing and within everyone's ability if you can be honest with yourself. Sometimes being honest with yourself is the most difficult part.

"The unexamined life is not worth living."

SOCRATES

The Predator

NONE OF US IS TRULY CONSCIOUS of who and what we are. We are learning and earning the right to see beyond the veil and 'know' once again. More enlightened beings can have glimpses of full consciousness, but full awareness has yet to be achieved on this earth plane unless you are one of the true Masters.

We are growing and experiencing all that the planes of consciousness have to offer, that is all of the realms of God's creation, so that we will once again come into full awareness of our Higher Selves. We are the highest of the high and the lowest of the low at the same time. Within our auric fields we encompass the full spectrum of consciousness on this plane. Our Higher Selves are of the higher levels of consciousness which have power and authority over the lower levels. Despite appearances and without exception, everything everywhere is in Divine Order.

> Despite appearances and without exception, everything everywhere is in Divine Order.

Your Higher Self is your personal deity, your Spirit, your God. It projected your soul to experience and to grow through the earthly material plane. Spirit and Soul are not interchangeable terms. The soul is seeking knowledge and experiences. The soul's growth is quicker on the earthly physical plane than it would be on the spiritual planes because it is working through many limitations that the spiritual planes do not have. Believe it or not, when it comes to spiritual growth, that's a good thing.

The Higher Self (Spirit) does not have the limitation of a physical body with only five senses. It does not have the limitation of the environment, a personality/ego, or the need for survival. In fact, the Higher Self does not have any limitations.

One thing I learned as this book was being dictated to me is that our Higher Selves do not have emotions. Emotions are strictly an earth plane phenomena that make the earth plane intoxicating and beneficial for spiritual growth. The Higher Self knows only love which is an energy, not an emotion as we commonly believe.

The way we recognize that energy and process it while we're in physical embodiment is usually through the body and the emotions. When that love vibrational energy is allowed to flow, most of us are aware of a lightness of being in the body. We lighten up! We experience joy. When we're 'in love' we release our emotional limitations and our Predator's need to control. Everything flows freely. We identify with and embrace that energy through sexual activity. It feels good and we sometimes take great risks to experience it as often as possible to recapture that feeling whether or not we 'love' the person.

Fear is the polarity of love. Our Predators fear everything especially our Higher Selves. Our Predators pull us in the opposite direction of our Higher Selves. Our thoughts are often influenced by our Predator. As thoughts are created in the mind, the brain processes them, and the Predator filters them through the emotions and experiences that we've picked up consciously and subconsciously. Our thoughts, energized by our emotions, manifest every day. Intense emotions can speed up the manifestation process for the good or for the bad. Your Higher Self (Spirit) and you are the co-creators of your life. When we are able to control our emotions and get into balance, we can manifest our desires on this earth plane more effectively like the Masters. (See the *Table of Emotions* in this book)

All of our incarnations have led us to this point. It is through the personalities (and egos) of those incarnations that we learned various perspectives and lessons. We identified ourselves through the Predator incarnations ago and we still do. We even deify our Predators by desiring fame, possessions and recognition to glorify them. It's like having our own reality television show. It's all about ego.

It is easy for us to get addicted to our emotions and dramas, after all, they are entertaining and make us feel alive. Our emotions are a tool we use to interpret our experiences and our lessons. It is hard to separate our true being from our personality and emotions, but that's part of the illusion of this earth plane.

> In the big picture, the Predator must die or at least be greatly humbled. It must learn to take a back seat to the Higher Self.

In the big picture, the Predator must die or at least be significantly humbled. It must learn to take a back seat to the Higher Self. Its demise is indicative of us uniting with our Higher Selves. It knows its death is imminent as we spiritually grow. However, as long as the Predator can keep us tied to our emotions and the seductive earthly experiences that separate us from our Higher Selves, it ensures itself a longer life, if not another incarnation or two (or three) of karma to transmute.

The Predator is afraid of dying because in the dying process your essence will be reunited into your Higher Self. It is set aside in the dying process and its usefulness ceases. But as long as our souls are learning from our struggles against the Higher Self, our strife will continue. The Higher Self has ultimate control over our lives. The quest to know our Higher Selves is a quest to 'Know Thyself' – your true self – not your Predator.

All of our internal and external battles have been between our Higher Selves and our Predators. The Higher Self created the circumstances for you to spiritually grow and the Predator repeatedly decided that it will have things its way and it doesn't need the Higher Self. Thus, we have the biblical allegory of the original sin in the Garden of Eden.

The Predator's needs and desires have no limit. Think of all the destruction that has taken place because of someone's need for wealth, control, and recognition to glorify their ego. A good example of the Predator's arrogance pertains to our own physical bodies. The Predator rejects our physical form that was perfectly designed by our Higher Selves for our karmic lessons. The Predator thinks the body needs changing to 'measure up'. The Predator needles you to change it. The Predator doesn't see the perfection in the Higher Self's creation and thinks it knows better. The Predator needs the approval of others. The Predator seeks and needs validation. The cosmetic industry knows this, as do plastic surgeons and retailers. There is a lot of money to be made catering to the Predator.

> The quest to know our Higher Selves is a quest to 'know thyself' – your true self – not your Predator.

The Predator reacts emotionally. The Predator makes us ambitious and desires recognition such as climbing the corporate ladder so it can legitimize itself as important and necessary when in actuality it is neither. Your Higher Self doesn't care about your status or ambitions. It only wants you to recognize it and become one with it. You are loved no more or no less by your Higher Self no matter what your circumstances are.

The Predator makes us buy things so that we can appear special, successful, and deserving of respect. It makes us jealous of others because it fears lack of recognition if it doesn't have the most enviable possessions. It needs an identity and the only way it can define itself is through the outside world by acquiring things like degrees, titles, possessions, etc. The more that our Predator acquires, the more it is clearly defined and has validation and form.

> Think of all the destruction that has taken place because of someone's need for wealth, control, and recognition to glorify their own ego.

The Predator has us believing that it makes our life easier and that it rescues us out of predicaments. The Predator is desperate for survival and has a stake in keeping us blind. As long as we think we are in control or are deep in the drama of an emotional abyss, we are blocked from our higher consciousness because the Predator has control.

Our true essence is an eternal spark of divine light. It has color and vibrates to a particular sound. It has a name known only to your Higher Self (Spirit) until you reach a higher level of consciousness when it will be revealed to you. You are not your personality/ego or your body. You are not your Predator.

How do you know when you've transmuted your Predator? You'll know when you no longer react to your dramas and see everything in Divine Order and/or when you no longer have a need to control. This is when your Higher Self reigns and the universe opens up. It is through the Universal Natural Laws you learn how to transmute the energy and let go of the earthly illusion.

"What lies behind us and what lies ahead of us are tiny matters compared to what lives within us."

HENRY DAVID THOREAU

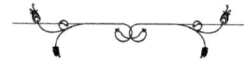

Ways of the Predator

At some point in our lives when things seem to be really out of control, we've all paused for a momentary reality check and asked ourselves 'how did I get to this point?' When the pain is too much to bear and we are finally ready to face the truth, it can be a cathartic moment where we step out of ourselves long enough to remember our past, see our present, and imagine a future that often doesn't look very pretty at the moment. This is a moment of clarity and we have to honestly answer the question: "Do you want to change your life or not?" What happens next is up to you but it is clearly time to have 'the talk' with your Predator.

The choice is yours to make as an individual and as part of the larger global community. The universe will support whatever you decide even if your decision is to do nothing but continue downward in a self-destructive spiral. Our individual choices matter to all of us because it creates a ripple effect in the lives of people that we know and even in the lives of many that we don't know. The Predator's negative energy is passed on in forms of crime, broken homes, insurance bills, litigation, divorce, shattered communities, fragmented governments, and crushed dreams. We all pay. What affects each individual, affects us all eventually.

Know that the fear of change can even make inaction seem like a good choice. Not to address our own issues is a choice.

How can we expect nations to be at peace when we as the individuals that make up those nations do not have peace within our own hearts? We all make up this global society but we pass the responsibility of peacemaking onto others with the expectation that someone else will make the first move. It is the responsibility of each of us. If the Predator continues to win, what will our world look like?

Everyone on the planet is connected on the spiritual realms even if having a body makes us appear separate. When one is in pain, we all suffer. The abused child that we ignore now grows into an angry, abusive adult that we will pay to incarcerate, medicate, counsel, or execute. Sometimes these adults become leaders and they bring their unresolved baggage with them into positions of authority. Then, the Predator gets a larger stage and the world pays on an even grander scale.

Think of all the people in your life that convinced you that you don't measure up in some way. You've probably been convinced during some encounter that you aren't smart enough, can't sing, dance, or fit in adequately. Someone somewhere convinced you that there is something inadequate about you and that sent you down the path of self-doubt. Marketing companies are paid billions to convince you that you are less than whole if you do not have their brands in your closet for every occasion, or that your body is too dark or needs tanning, or that aging is a crime rather than an honor or at the very least an acceptable, natural part of life. These perceptions trivialize you and the noble Spirit that you are. Question the Predator. Question your actions and your thoughts. Ask yourself, 'Why do I spend time on such shallowness?' What are your actual needs versus the desires that the Predator motivates you to chase?

The truth is that we are limitless. What is holding us back are our beliefs. Our battle isn't with the people around us. Our battle isn't with institutions or bosses that have perceived authority over us. The only battle that we are fighting is the battle within us – the Predator. Those people are merely actors helping us to become consciously aware of what is going on within us. They are our mirrors. They are playing a role in this game called life just for us. It's a valuable experience and Leonard Michaelson (Spirit Guide) said that 'we learn best through trial and error, and fastest through pain'. We are indeed in a school called Earth and we are its students.

It is easier to let other people think for us because we respect others more than we respect ourselves. We let loved ones think for us. We let people with perceived authority make life decisions for us. Belittling our abilities is one way the Predator keeps control. It undermines the Spirit. Letting others think for us is how we get out of taking responsibility for our decisions and for the outcomes of those decisions. However, our ability to clearly think for ourselves is fundamental to our ability to create and attract good to us. It is the basis of personal power. We have to be present, conscious, and balanced in our own lives to be effective in it. God gave us all the freedom to choose our path. However, we have to accept the responsibility that goes along with that freedom.

> Why are you convinced that someone else will look out for your needs and nurture your dreams better than you can?

How many ways have you given away our personal power to someone else? How many times have you been disappointed in the outcome when you let someone make a decision for you or take control of your affairs? Why are you convinced that someone else will look out for your needs and nurture your dreams better than you can? Love is the energy behind your personal power. We all have unlimited access to that God-power. When used correctly it is the most revitalizing force imaginable. If we hand over our personal power to someone else, we can expect to be disappointed repeatedly. **It is your power and not to be given away – especially not to the Predator!** You have to wield it correctly. Again, love is not an emotion. It is energy. It is God's energy.

Before we can resolve anything, we have to be conscious of what motivates us, especially our fears. Fear is paralyzing. Oftentimes we bury our fears to the point that we aren't even aware of them. We travel through life never really feeling alive or at peace. What we've experienced in life has taught us to fear, to doubt ourselves, to feel separate from God, and to embrace a consciousness of helplessness and deprivation. Fear is the Predator's motivator. Your Spirit fears nothing. The wonderful thing about this is that once we've experienced the depths of a so-called hell, and we've learned the lesson, we now have earned the right to experience what the heights of heaven on Earth can be. The pendulum does indeed swing the other way (and it's a Natural Law).

The Natural Law of Rhythm (*The Kybalion by the Three Initiates*) states that the negative swing of the pendulum is equal to the positive swing of the pendulum. (I vaguely remember that concept from one of my rather dull physics classes in college. We had to calculate the pendulum's swing. Glad to know all of my college education wasn't a total waste!)

Our imaginations and desires are our keys, but it begins by imagining and desiring a different vision first of ourselves, and then for ourselves. You'll have to go against your Predator who is fearful. Look around. Everything, every circumstance, and everyone in your environment was attracted to you through your present state of consciousness. Do you like what you see?

That disconnect from our Higher Selves that the Predator relies upon makes us feel vulnerable and we may react by having a need to control everyone and everything in our lives – making us control freaks. We may buy unnecessary things to placate our fears in order to feel an elusive state of safety and control. If we still can't get our immediate needs met, we may choose to mask the pain, even if only for a few minutes, through destructive means or instigate situations that make us feel more powerful and in control.

We won't be able to buy enough clothes, electronic gadgets, food, drugs, or booze to fill that void in our hearts. No amount of money can make us really feel safe because we know it can all be taken away in an instant and we'll find ourselves left again with another opportunity to face yet another fear. What fears are you trying to avoid facing? How long do you think you can avoid it? Forever is not the correct answer.

> In crises your Predator is being humbled so that you can look at your situation in a different way.
> CHERUB CORNELIUS

Fear is an interesting concept. I can remember being intrigued by a passage I read some time ago that stated that you cannot master fear. You must master love to resolve fear. It's true. We cannot directly combat a fear in order to overcome it. No one ever has, per se. Nevertheless, at our disposal we have the personal power to love. Love and fear cannot occupy the same space and time. You have to find the strength that love (self-love) awakens within us to face and question the validity of the fear, ultimately dissolving it and the illusion. Finding love is done by consciously connecting to our inner guidance and tapping into that reservoir of strength. In other words, love yourself enough to tap into your inner strength to challenge and overcome the fear. Let the Predator lose the battle. Reach higher. Will you let the Predator or your Spirit guide you?

When we are truly ready to change our thinking for the better and take responsibility for our lives, the personality/ego has to be humbled so new thoughts can create a new beginning. The All, God, has never used material possessions or money to demonstrate favoritism of one person or group over another. God has never loved any one of us more than the next. How can God love one part of his/herself more than the other? To think so is nonsense and locks us into limited, judgmental thinking. In one channeled session, the Spirit Guide Iris stated, "God doesn't care what position or status you have in your earthly life. Everyone is equal and those conditions are only there as vehicles for the purpose of growth."

Dedicating our lives to acquiring money and possessions is based on faulty thinking. It is a strong indication that your Predator has firm control over you. Money and possessions can come as a result of your humanitarian or spiritual pursuits but if it is your main goal, you're creating lessons for yourself. In such cases, crises may develop such as money problems or disease at the very height of your accomplishments. It is part of the lesson to get your attention so that you can discern what is really important. In crises we learn what is important quickly. If we are wise and ready, we will quickly open our hearts to new ideas and new beginnings. Eventually, new people will enter our lives aiding us on our new path once we have turned away from the old. It is part of the unfolding process of spiritual development.

> Suppose all that you've worked for and accumulated isn't what your Spirit wants for you?

My Spirit Guide Carmen stated to the group in a channeled session, "The pursuit of money and your fascination with your bodies and inventions have divided humans and led you away from God just like in Atlantis. Earth changes, government crises…and shortages will make you return and embrace what is important in your lives and get you back to the basics. For that to which you have become accustomed to will change. Humans will again search for strength within and that connection to God." The 2008 financial crisis indeed presented us with that challenge. Growing world water shortages are causing tension amongst neighboring countries. According to Carmen, there is much more to come with the Earth changes.

Suppose all that you've worked for and accumulated isn't what your Spirit wants for you? What if your Spirit wants to take you in another direction? Our Spirit knows exactly what will make us happy and what will open our hearts with joy. Our Spirit isn't depriving us of joy when we don't get exactly what we think we want. Spirit is continuously leading us to our joy. Oftentimes we only see what we're losing and not what good is coming to us. If you're in a crisis, what will it take for you to let go of your attachment to your things, including some people, in order to find true happiness built on a strong, stable foundation?

It is a choice that we all make at some point in our lives — to change or not to change. How do we trust the unknown even when we know deep within that whatever lies ahead has to be better than the present situation? How do we let go and trust our inner guidance? Usually the pain of the lesson has to be unbearable before we make that leap of faith. But, it doesn't have to be painful. Our fears hold us back, separating us from the unlimited potential of our Spirit. Again, fear is the Predator's primary weapon for control.

What has to happen before we decide we've had enough? How much pain do we have to endure before we choose to accept something better? My Spirit Guides told me and the class on several occasions to stop fighting our Higher Selves. The answer is simply a change in our thinking. Stop defending our point of view and ego long enough to look at what we are doing to ourselves and those around us to keep that point of view. When we initiate a change in consciousness, the universe will respond. It begins with our thoughts, our consciousness. It all begins mentally.

No matter what your situation is, all your thoughts, beliefs, words, and deeds got you to this point. Each day we take responsibility by experiencing them firsthand as individuals and as a collective consciousness. We are verifying their truth by living them out in our own lives. This means both the good and the bad. Once we experience them, we can then change our thinking based on that experience.

Karma comes to us when we do something contrary to our spiritual selves. During a channeled session, Iris defined karma as unlearned lessons. For example, when we condemn or judge ourselves and others, it is the one that judges that reaps the karma. It may not return immediately, but it will return. When we think and speak of ourselves or others in negative, limiting, or unforgiving terms, we insult Spirit which is perfect in every way. How would you like those self-condemning thoughts to manifest at your next job interview by being told that you aren't smart enough, young enough, or that you don't look the part? (Remember, the interviewer is only playing a role for you to learn the lesson.)

My Cherub Cornelius stated, "When you are at rock bottom, feeling defeated and disillusioned, that is when you are most open to something new. Your current thoughts, that judgment that you defended, that criticism that you identified with so strongly, that opinion that resonated with you so well, have all failed you. In crises you are being humbled so that you can look at your situation in a different way. You are being humbled so that you can be more compassionate with yourself and others and to learn not to judge." We don't have to go through a crises to learn, although it seems to be the preferred way by humans.

Have you ever noticed how many judgments you can make in one day? If you want to learn something about yourself, take one day to jot down each time you criticize someone or have a judgmental thought. Take lots of paper. Count them at the end of the day. This includes judgments of yourself as well as others. These are your subconscious thoughts percolating to the surface in the words that you speak, and are often reflected in the things that you do. The positive ones don't have the unpleasant karmic effect like the intensely negative ones that haunt us for incarnations. Nevertheless, you are responsible for every one of your thoughts, beliefs, words, and deeds. Scary isn't it? Judgements have scary consequences especially if you persist.

> You are responsible for every one of your thoughts, beliefs, words, and deeds. Scary isn't it?

Cornelius never skirted an issue. He always got to the heart of the matter no matter how much it hurt, but we were all the better for his honesty and directness. My ego was bruised several times when he taught classes. He expected a lot out of his future teachers. You can't protect a fragile ego when Spirit Guides are around. They know the truth about you and they know what you're thinking when you think it. I understand now that it was the only way to shatter the illusion and the perceived power of my Predator. I'm very grateful for the experience.

You may be wondering what the difference between a fact and a judgment is. Iris explained it this way: "A fact states the condition that is evident without emotion, such as the observation that a 700 lb. man is obese. Is a 700 lb. man obese in comparison to other humans on your planet? Yes, that is a fact. However, a judgment condemns according to your beliefs and fears and doesn't see the perfection in the lessons yet to be learned by the 700 lb. man that are necessary for his spiritual growth." Her comment made me stop and think about my own condemnations of others and to become more aware of my own thinking on a daily basis. It made a big difference!

"In losing control, you gain control. Balance is where you will find peace."

Omar Khayyam

Humbling the Predator

TAKE A DEEP BREATH AND RELAX for a few moments. Close your eyes. Let your imagination take you to a safe place. Then ask yourself, "What is happiness for me?" Meditate on that statement and see what you come up with.

Happiness has different definitions depending upon what stage of life we are in and if our basic needs have been met. If we define happiness in material terms like a new car or a 5,000 sq. ft. home, we are only looking at temporary happiness. Once we possess those items, we will soon be looking once again to fill the emptiness of the Predator.

Materialism is the kind of happiness that our Predator desires, not your Spirit. It defines itself by possessions and compares you to others. It cultivates envy and negative competition. When we buy into that illusion and define ourselves and our self-worth by those things, we set ourselves up for a disappointing karmic life lesson in order to learn what real happiness is. Look at the sacrifices we make to maintain ownership of those possessions such as high debt and time away from family and friends to earn money to keep those possessions. And yet, those 'things' can be taken away in an instant.

Real happiness that is long lasting and meaningful comes from our alignment with our Spirit. Yes, we will still have 'things' but those 'things' will no longer define us or stroke our egos. They will just be what they are meant to be - things. The truth is that once we connect with our Spirit, we won't desire the materialism on this Earth plane that seduces so many at such a high moral and high spiritual cost. The desire for material things seems to die off. What you actually need will always be provided.

Don't get me wrong. It is absolutely fine to have possessions. They make living comfortable on Earth. However, they shouldn't be our motivation in life. This void can only be filled by consciously recognizing that we and our Spirits are one. The 'stuff', if we still want it, will follow.

To get to the point of happiness, we usually have to do some house cleaning so that the past doesn't drain energy from the future we are consciously creating. Some have had more to do than others (me!) but regardless, the house cleaning has to be done no matter how unpleasant the task.

You don't have to do all of it before you start to consciously create your future, but at the very least starting the process opens up a lot of doors because your thinking has changed. But you know that. So why hang on to your pain? Is it because the pain is comfortable and familiar? Is it the fear of the void that will be created if you let go? Is it the fear of losing something that has become a part of you? Is it the fear that if you get rid of one thing, there's an avalanche of other things behind it that you aren't ready to deal with? If the answer is yes to any of those questions, the first thing to do is to forgive yourself for the mistakes of the past so that healing the past will be easier. You did the best that you could with what you knew at the time. Today, it's a different story. You know better. You've learned the lesson. Now it's time to move on. Don't let the Predator keep control over you.

During an interview, Michael Bernard Beckwith, founder of the Agape International Spiritual Center, stated, "Forgiveness is giving up the hope that things could have been different." This is our key to freedom. We cannot change the past but we can stop it from paralyzing our present and destroying our future. We don't have to forget or make excuses for anyone's behavior. Nor do we have to somehow convince ourselves that the event didn't take place or that what happened is now acceptable. We do, however, have to accept that it happened, forgive ourselves and the people concerned, and understand what the lesson brought to us. Then, we have to release the emotions tied to it so that we can move on. This is no small task.

It took years for me to forgive the man that raped me – a literal Predator. But I knew I had a choice. I could live with the pain of the horrific memory and literally rehash it every day for the rest of my life or I could free myself from those chains and claim a better life for myself. I chose the latter.

Michael Bernard Beckwith, founder of the Agape International Spiritual Center, stated, "Forgiveness is giving up the hope that things could have been different."

Changing the energy of a situation is called transmutation and the power to do that is yours. It is a choice you have to make.

That encounter taught me that I am stronger than anything that can happen to me and in the process, he strengthened my spiritual beliefs. I no longer carry around the anger that I had for him. That anger was killing me, not him. It was like being victimized twice. I had to release myself from those shackles because no one else could.

When we get obsessed with our pain or a hurt from the past, we miss new doors of opportunity, further punishing ourselves. You will want to let it go because when the mind is enslaved, anything you create reflects that fear-based negative energy, even as disease in our bodies. The ability to forgive requires the strength that love makes available to us. That is what loving ourselves is about - letting go of what is not needed.

Ask yourself, 'What is the highest and best for me?' The first step is to find balance within ourselves. Meditation is our key. It takes practice and perseverance, somewhat akin to exercising, but it is well worth the effort. I'm not a fan of stomach crunches but I'll stop and meditate anywhere. I think of it as a spiritual exercise for the Soul. It is the more desirable way to tame the Predator. It is a mindful, conscious process. The mental and spiritual clarity that meditation produces grants us the objectivity needed to experience the earth plane illusion without getting lost in it.

Meditation is not optional for those on a conscious spiritual path. With practice it will quiet the mind and give you a peaceful break from your day. It raises our consciousness in order to reach a point of balance and communication. More people are discovering its benefits and are embracing it. But you know that too. So why is it hard for people to do it regularly?

> The peace that you have in your life is a reflection of the peace that you have in your heart.

It is because the Predator does not want you to meditate. That is why spiritual teachers will insist that students learn to meditate and do it on a regular basis. It humbles the Predator. Students that do not or refuse to discipline their egos enough to meditate will eventually take a different, more earthly path and become disillusioned before returning to the spiritual path. Being sidetracked is common. It may take several incarnations for some to get back to their spiritual path, but the good news is that everyone will return. The more painful your experiences, the more devoted the student will be when they return to the spiritual path. That's called learning a karmic lesson. It's the story of the prodigal son.

The less desirable method to tame the Predator is the earthly path filled with ego lessons. Never let it be said that pain and humiliation are not motivators or at the very least humbling.

A bruised ego hurts and we will do anything to alleviate the pain. I can attest to that as I'm sure others can.

There has to be a strong desire to know your true self (your Spirit) if you are to tame the Predator. You have to think clearly in order to do that, which means thinking without the Predator's influence. Iris (Spirit Guide) told us this world is full of weak-minded thinkers that are easily swayed and led astray. This is true especially in dealing with spiritual matters. She stated that it is easier to have someone tell us what to do rather than think it through for ourselves and follow our own inner guidance. That weak-mindedness is your Predator wanting you to have more faith in this earth plane existence than in the spiritual path to your Higher Self. It is true that we can grow in the dark or in ignorance, so to speak, and we have for many, many incarnations. However, being conscious, awake, and aware (self-aware) of our spiritual development is the path of the Master, which we are all aspiring to be – consciously or not. No matter which route we take to get there, all routes lead back to The All - God. You can't go wrong, but why take the longer, pain filled route?

Look at the Predator as a learning tool that takes us out of balance. Omar Khayyam stated in a channeled session, "In order to gain control, we first have to lose control." In other words, we recognize balance when we experience both sides of the pendulum. In times of crises, we don't recognize that easily. "Balance is where you will find peace", according to Omar. That is where our power lies.

Staying in balance is the challenge. We cannot effectively create or be truly free unless we are at a point of balance, which is when our energy and the energy of our Spirit are in alignment. At that point, you'll just know. I can't describe it to you. There are no words that can give you a clear description of that state. You'll just know.

When we are out of balance we struggle against that energy and create chaos and karma. We can transmute the energy of undesirable situations by raising it to the highest and best energy that we can through our thoughts, words and deeds, and then move on. That is why this plane of conscious is known as a school. We are learning, or better stated, re-learning that which we already know but have forgotten. We are Spirit. We are being awakened to that fact. How quickly or slowly that awakening occurs is up to us. No matter what we've done, no matter how worthless we have been told that we are, we are still progressing and will continue to progress.

How do we let go and move on? We put one foot in front of the other and keep walking and meeting the challenges placed in front of us as honestly and as positively as we can, no matter how the circumstances look at the time. Trust the Spirit within you to guide you. Ask for Spirit's guidance when you need it. Spirit will guide us even if we don't ask.

A good thing to have would be patience. First we have to find patience for ourselves somewhere, somehow. Too bad we can't purchase patience in a bottle and use it when we need it. That would be a worthwhile purchase along with a good chocolate cheesecake. Women will understand that statement.

Our Higher Self really wants us to recognize it, to join with it, and to willingly give up the Predator. In other words, stop being entertained by the Predator and stop the pull against the Higher Self. That scenario never ends well and causes our daily pain. When we give up the struggle and the pull against the Higher Self, everything gets easier. The stress ceases. You can feel the stress being released in your body. When we stop the pull we are handing over control to the Higher Self. Until then, we will stay where we are, experiencing our fears and trying to control everything around us. When we come into alignment with our Spirit, and the Predator has been humbled, we will know true freedom. Until then, the ride is rather bumpy. But, your Spirit will wait for you.

The Table of Emotional Understanding

ON THE NEXT FEW PAGES is a table of emotions and the Predator's need at the time of the emotion. Understanding emotions will help you to understand and control the ego. Being conscious of your experiences and emotions is key.

In each circumstance, keep asking yourself 'why' until you get down to the real fear. Ask your Spirit Guides to show you your ego and then be alert to the people that show up, their attitudes, and how they interact with you. They are your mirrors. Take note of your experiences over the next few days as you work on each emotion. Journal it. Meditate on it. Keep doing this every time you emotionally react and you will see a pattern emerge. Some emotions require more work than others depending on how deep they are and your history, but you are worth the effort!

Find the emotion that you are experiencing on the table below and read what the Predator (ego) is experiencing at the time of the emotion. Once you are conscious of your patterns, you can change them if you desire. I hope you find this guide useful as a reference in your daily life.

Anger	Ego identity and current perceptions have been threatened; holding on to current circumstances and thought patterns; refusing change
Annoyed	Striving to create and control the outcome but finding the progress and/or outcome unacceptable
Anxious	Fear of being judged and being vulnerable; fear of the unknown; fear of the current or impending lack of control
Bored	Needing to create events to further define the ego; fear of internalizing truth
Conceit	Deification of the ego; ego self-worship; placing utmost importance in the physical illusion
Confused	Lack of willingness to accept guidance from higher sources; the ego realizes it doesn't have the solution

The Table of Emotional Understanding

Courageous	Your ability to challenge the ego in order to face your fears; willingness to recognize the illusion despite the ego
Creative	(Positive) Expression of the Higher-Self through the balanced ego. (Negative) Expression of the lower-self through an unbalanced fear-filled ego.
Critical	Focused need to dictate surroundings and circumstances to suit the ego regardless of others; needing to control and influence others; imposing (sense of self-important) desires on others to feel superior - usually condescending in nature
Depression	The ego has lost its identity and is seeking a new earthly identity that may be just as faulty; refusal to seek guidance from the Higher Self; refusal to let go of the past; needing attention and validation from outside sources
Eager	Need to dictate Divine Order; See 'Impatience'
Escapism	Resulting activities due to the ego's inability to accept the current circumstances as they are and the refusal to change; victim mentality (See 'Victim')
Ecstasy	Often referred to as a state of Nirvana; the experience of total bliss without the limitations of the ego and physical plane; rising above the earthly illusion (See 'Happiness')

Failure	Your ego has identified itself with its creation and judged it unacceptable; desperately lost in the illusion
Fear	The polarity of love resulting from the ego's reluctant awareness that it has no control of its destiny and its existence is tenuous; not willing to acknowledge (or rise to) the power of your Higher Self - your true being
Frightened	Ego's recognition of the unknown and lack of control over it
Frustrated	The ego's inability to define itself adequately in the outer world
Greed	The ego's identity is not well defined; needing excess to secure its identity and status. Belief that with ownership and possessions comes control. Must constantly seek the material in order to nurture the fearful ego incessantly; disbelief in an abundant universe
Guilt	Recognizing the reality that following the Higher-Self (your inner voice) would have yielded better results
Happiness	Living in the moment without fear or suffering; recognizing your oneness with your Higher Self knowing you lack nothing; being whole (See 'Ecstasy')

Hatred	An ego witnessing some reflection of itself and the need to destroy it
Helpless	Broad recognition that the ego in reality has absolutely no control; refusal to seek help from the Higher Self; feeling vulnerable
Humiliation	(See 'Shame')
Impatience	Misuse of the will in order to manipulate and control; mistrust of the Natural Law of Divine Order
Indecisive	(See 'Confused')
Inflexible	The ego's dire need to be correct and to control others; holding on to your truth perspective
Insecurity	Feeling that what has been acquired and currently identified with will be taken away (See 'Anxious')
Inspired	Creativity channeled from the Higher Self; feeling connected to that vast creative source
Intolerant	Hiding the fear of inadequacy by projecting superiority and dominance (See 'Inflexible')

Irritated	(See 'Annoyed')
Isolated	Separating parts of self; an ego's need to be correct and unwilling to consider another perspective in order to protect itself
Jealous	Fear of losing, or inability to obtain something or someone of value prompting feelings of inadequacy and lack
Joy	Tamed ego that identifies with the Higher-Self and the Master plan (See 'Happiness')
Judgmental	Creating self-defined limitations imposed on self and/or others; desire for authority and dominion over others in order to control (See 'Critical')
Love	The highest energy vibration in the universe resulting from a balanced ego and the union with the Higher Self; honoring the God within self, another, and in all things; polarity of fear; it is not an emotion – it is an energy
Lust	Needing to experience sexual energy on the physical plane while ignoring the spiritual element of the sexual union (See 'Greed')

Moody	Needing attention; desiring a sense of importance for validation (See 'Isolated' and 'Frustrated')
Overwhelmed	Misuse of power and insistence on controlling; too much importance placed in the physical plane illusion; inability to let go and trust the universe
Pain	A way to use the body to punish yourself for suppressed thoughts and emotions
Patient	Turning over the need to control to your Higher Self and the recognition that the Universal Natural Laws are working in your life for your highest evolvement; belief in Divine Order
Pessimistic	Unwillingness to put aside ego in order to connect to your Higher Self for guidance
Pleasure	Recognition of truth and merging into the oneness (See 'Happiness')
Powerless	(See 'Victim')
Pride	Can be good or bad depending upon the balance or state of the ego - happiness with the ego self and its creations, or an overly exaggerated sense of self-worth and power masking the feeling of inferiority; ego's attempt to associate its identity with the material plane

Rage	(See 'Anger')
Rebellious	An ego's determined desire to have control and recognition but will always be frustrated by truth and the Higher Self
Rejection	Probably the most devastating to the ego - the outside world has judged the ego's identity as unacceptable and/or inadequate
Remorse	Ego tormenting and judging itself; recognizing its vulnerabilities (See 'Guilt')
Repressed	Fear of the power of the Higher-Self (your true self); ego asserting control
Resentful	Injured egoic expression as it recognizes that it has no control or power; recognition that a higher authority (the Higher Self) has all of the control
Responsible	A mature, balanced ego's accountability for the conception, nurturing, and outcome of all thoughts, words and deeds past and present
Revenge	Needing to punish and/or destroy challenges to the ego's identity or existence
Scared	(See 'Fear' and 'Frightened')

Selfishness	The ego's need to attract attention, support, and resources without the consideration of others; ego's self-attempt at validation
Shame	The resulting vulnerability of an ego's identity that has been exposed, controlled, criticized, and/or judged ethically or morally unacceptable by self or society
Sorrow	The inability to control the past
Stubborn	Needing to have control over surroundings or people to passive-aggressively assert dominance
Surprise	Can be positive or negative – an ego recognizing and assessing an unpredictable event (or threat) outside your current realm of thinking or power
Sympathy	Being able to emotionally connect to the ego lesson of another person or group
Trust	True recognition and acceptance that the Universal Natural Laws are always in effect for your highest good; lack of need to control self or others knowing that everything is unfolding as it should; certainty and belief in the support of your Higher Self

Unclean	Judging self for a breach of personal boundaries imposed by self, society, or other outside forces. Punishing self with sexual guilt or remorse, usually resulting from uncontrollable (unexpected) events; a negative ego centered self-image
Vanity	(See 'Conceit')
Victim	Ego judging self as prey, weak, powerless, and/or inferior in order to separate oneself from the Higher Self to justify its existence; deceptive justification for being separate from the Higher Self; one's perceived sacrifice did not lead to a desirable result
Vulnerable	Ego's fear of exposure and lacking adequate protection to shield itself; fear of powerlessness; inability to corroborate or rationalize emotional confusion
Worry	Inability to control an outcome of a situation or the response of others

The Balanced Ego

I'VE SPENT A LOT OF TIME writing about the negative side of the ego — which my Spirit teachers called our Predator. However, when it is in balance it isn't destructive. Quite the contrary is true. For example, we probably get a good feeling by doing volunteer work and helping others that seem less fortunate. Remember something — not only are the less fortunate giving us the opportunity to be of service, but they too are going through their ego lessons by letting us be of service to them. Everyone is working on ego issues.

A balanced ego knows the higher spiritual plan is being worked out despite the appearances of negativity, wars, poverty, hatred, etc. A balanced ego observes the Universal Natural Law of Divine Order being instituted in all that is going on and doesn't need to compete or control anyone or anything. A balanced ego sees God in everything and in everyone. A balanced ego has no fear.

A balanced ego doesn't need more money than what is necessary to exist on the physical plane. A balanced ego doesn't define itself in materialistic terms. It is interesting that the material things come in abundance when you don't need or want them. The desire for possessions, wealth, fame, validation, and control diminish. It's the earth plane experience that teaches the ego to desire more substantial things in this universe — such as love and to know itself as God. A balanced ego won't idealize the body or think of the body as being anything more than a vehicle for learning, communicating, and experiencing the earth plane through the five senses.

Iris stated, "It's good to feel the pain. The Predator will give up. When the Predator cries, the Spirit celebrates." It celebrates because the Predator is willing to let go because of the pain. The ego is being diminished allowing the Higher Self to reign. It is a spiritual victory on the road to a higher consciousness. Despite appearances, everyone wins.

Remember that your Higher Self — God — still loves you no matter who you are, no matter what you've done, and always will. Know that!

"Not till we are completely lost or turned around… do we begin to find ourselves."

HENRY DAVID THOREAU

Exercise 1: Working With Your Emotions

Emotions are projections from the personality/ego – your Predator. If you want to see how strong your Predator's grip is on you, take one week and make a list of all your intensely negative emotions and fears in the space below. Use more paper if necessary. See how your emotions (your ego) keep you from your own personal power. See how they paralyze you. Do the same with resentments. Notice the patterns. Behavioral patterns are important. Once you are conscious of your patterns and fears, understanding them empowers you and mitigates the fear. Use the *Table of Emotional Understanding* in this book to see what your ego wants and what your emotions mean. You can then decide objectively what the best course of action is for you.

> **Example**: 'I get <u>angry</u> when my boyfriend <u>criticizes</u> me."
>
> Look up 'anger' and 'critical' in the *Table of Emotional Understanding* and note that your boyfriend threatens your current perception of yourself as he imposes his personal limitations on you for control.
>
> Now ask yourself, why is his opinion more important than yours?
>
> Have you given your personal power over to him?
>
> Since everyone in your life is a mirror to some extent, where have you been critical of others? Be honest about it.
>
> Where else does this occur in your life? Watch for patterns.
>
> What fear do you have, become conscious of it, and determine what you have to lose if you confront the fear?

Exercise 2: What Do You Think of Yourself?

Make a list of all your faults. Be honest about what you think about yourself. Include all of the things that you don't like about yourself. Don't edit it — just write what you think at the time. Do this over the next week or longer until it feels complete. When you think you're done, categorize your list. They could be categories such as my body, my personality, failures, or my abilities, etc. See how your Predator undermines your God-self. See where you need to work on your ego. Now, write about your perceived good qualities over a week's period and again categorize them. Note the pattern.

Why do you consider one trait as 'good' and another trait as 'bad'? Bottom line, you'll have to love both sides of yourself unconditionally. It's part of the process of acceptance for what is.

_____

_____

_____

Exercise 2: What Do You Think of Yourself?

Other Works by the Author in the WISDOM FROM SPIRIT GUIDES series:

"What Happens Next Is Up To You"
"Healing the Human Ego"

Seminar and Webinar Topics
Beginning Meditation
Karma & Reincarnation
Beginning and Intermediate Astrology
Spiritual Anatomy
Spirit Guides
The Universal Natural Laws
Reiki (All Levels)
Your Personal Forecast for the Coming Year
The Astrological Forecast for the US
Death & Dying
Energy & Vibration
Self-Awareness
Prayer Techniques

And many more!

Audio / Video / Webinars / Online Resources

Go to www.thelightofourbeing.org

Like us on Facebook:
https://www.facebook.com/wisdomfromspiritguides

Email: lynn@lynnwalker.org

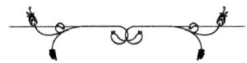

"Mind is ever the ruler of the universe."

Plato

www.ingramcontent.com/pod-product-compliance
Lightning Source LLC
Chambersburg PA
CBHW061253040426
42444CB00010B/2377